A Photographic Journey down

ECCLESALL ROAD

from Whirlow to Town

Published by **Arc Publishing and Print**

166 Knowle Lane, Bents Green, Sheffield S11 9SJ.

t: 07809 172872 w: www.sheffieldbooks.co.uk

Acknowledgements

Many thanks to the following people who supplied photographs and information for this book.

Roger Pepper

Russell Peckett

Roger Taylor

Don Alexander

Paul Iseard

David Richardson

Shirley Frost

Jane Salt at Sheffield Newspapers

Margaret and Ronny Hindmoor

Brenda Keeling

Gordon Ramsey

Winifred Wilson

Maurice and Mabel Cooke

Barbara Tyler

Special thanks to the staff at Sheffield Central Library, Local Studies Department for permission to reproduce photographs from their collection.

Text copyright 2009 © Chris Keeling

The rights of Chris Keeling and his work has been asserted by him in accordance with the
Copyright, Design Patent Act 1988

November 2009

ISBN: 978-1-906722-13-5

Published by Arc Publishing and Print
166 Knowle Lane
Sheffield
S11 9SJ

Telephone 07809 172872

This book is dedicated to the late
William Michael Glossop Keeling

Introduction

Many people may think this book should have started in the city centre and ended at Whirlow, but I always think of travelling into town down Ecclesall Road. So I began my journey at Whirlow - a lovely area on the outskirts of Sheffield - close to the Peak District National Park. It is Ecclesall Road South from Whirlow to Banner Cross, where it drops the South and becomes Ecclesall Road. It winds its way along four and a quarter miles from the edge of the Derbyshire countryside, through wealthy suburbs, busy shopping areas and into the heart of the city. Ecclesall Road has been, and still is, one of the busiest roads in and out of Sheffield. Some parts of the road have changed little over the last 120 years but the bottom of Ecclesall Road has changed beyond recognition and not for the better in my opinion. Why did they destroy so many beautiful buildings? Some dates mentioned are approximate and I apologize in advance for any mistakes.
I have enjoyed gathering together these old photographs - some dating back to the 1890's and others more recent. This book will hopefully bring back many memories of what I call 'The Road to Town'.
I hope you enjoy the journey.

Index

Whirlow to Parkhead

1. Whirlow Bridge Inn

2. Scrat Houses

3. Broomcroft

4. Parkhead House

5. 380 Ecclesall Road South 'Mona Ville'

6. Mrs Binny's House on Abbey Lane

7. Wheatsheaf Inn

8. Parkhead Cottages

9. George Greenfields Post Office

Map date 1905

5

Ecclesall Road South

The junction of Hathersage Road and Ecclesall Road South at Whirlow Bridge. Whirlow Bridge Inn was built in 1846 on the old turnpike road. This double fronted building was originally a beer house with stabling at the side. It was frequented by many a walker who enjoyed the rural walk from the city.

The pub was turned into tea rooms after the landlord lost his licence. It later become a private house but was demolished in August 1938 to make way for two stone built houses.

This is the original road sign at the start of Ecclesall Road South and can still be found on the old road near the entrance to Whirlow Brook Park.

This stretch of road where Ecclesall Road South meets Hathersage Road became very busy in the 1950's as more and more people owned their own cars.

After numerous accidents on this dangerous bend of the old turnpike road, the road was eventually straightened. The lodge in the background belongs to Whirlow Brook Park.

Aerial view before the road was straightened.

These three cottages on the next bend of the road at 480 - 482 were called Scrat Houses. Named after the "Scrat" a wild shaggy wood sprite!! They were occupied for many years by the Osbourne family and demolished around 1970 due possibly to their proximity to the bend in the road. If you look carefully you can still see evidence today of these Scrat Houses in a portion of the wall.

Parkhead House - formerly The Woodlands was in an area known as St Ann's in the middle of the 19th century. It was designed by a young Sheffield architect in 1864 called John Mitchell-Withers. He lived there with his family. It was sold in 1898 to Robert Hadfield who renamed it Parkhead House.

Broomcroft - Wealthy engineer and boiler maker David Davy commissioned John Mitchell-Withers to design Broomcroft which sits in large grounds across the road from Parkhead House. It has now been turned into a nursing home.

Walter Ramsey bought 'Broomcroft' at Parkhead. It was a magnificent house, now a care home for the elderly, but his wife Annie refused to live there because she said it was too large. The land that came with the house extended as far as Parkhead Road. Walter developed this land which included an imposing house for himself called 'Mona Villa', 380 Ecclesall Road South, where he lived until his death in 1942.

Walter's son Alan was also a builder and completed the development of the Broomcroft land, by building all the houses on Parkhead Road. The advert proof from the Sheffield Telegraph below promotes Parkhead as 'Derbyshires Beautiful Gateway'.

SUNSHINE HOMES AT DERBYSHIRE'S BEAUTIFUL GATEWAY: ECCLESALL ROAD SOUTH & PARKHEAD ROAD.

Houses as illustrated (in course of construction) with Four Bedrooms **£875**

Three-Bedroomed Houses in Parkhead Road. From **£650**

Glass Panelled Bathrooms and Lavatory.
Tiled Kitchens.
Oak Panelled Halls.
Room for Garage.
Every House Plastered in Patent Thistle Plaster (no lime) which eliminates cracked ceilings, etc.
Planned to give you lasting pleasure.
Decorated to your taste.
A House you will be proud to own.

ALLAN RAMSAY, CONTRACTOR, Phone: PARKHEAD. ECCLESALL ROAD SOUTH, SHEFFIELD.

The Wheatsheaf in 1908 and as it is today.

Walter Ramsay was a keen supporter of Parkhead Cricket Club just across the road from his house and in 1940 he was elected president of the club (see Heap cartoon).

Even though motor cars were common place in the 1930's, people still went to the Wheatsheaf in their pony and trap.

The top of Abbey Lane is on the right and the old Wheatsheaf pub in the distance. Note that Park Head Road and Park Head Crescent have not yet been built.

Mrs Binny standing in the doorway of her cottage on Abbey lane, just off Ecclesall Road. c1930. Now Demolished.

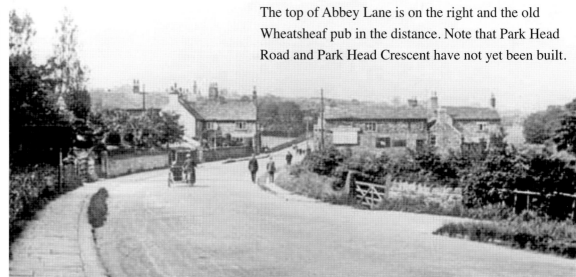

Front of Postcard

Wheatsheaf, early 1900

This post card was produced for the Wheatsheaf Cavalier Steak House in 1980 It shows the pub in the early 1900s. Many people took up this very generous offer as we were in a recession, sounds familiar!

Reverse of Postcard

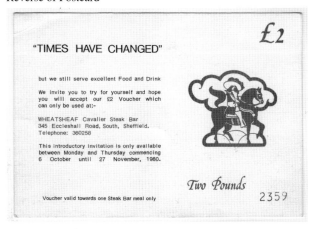

"TIMES HAVE CHANGED"

but we still serve excellent Food and Drink

We invite you to try for yourself and hope you will accept our £2 Voucher which can only be used at:-

WHEATSHEAF Cavalier Steak Bar
345 Ecclesall Road, South, Sheffield.
Telephone: 360258

This introductory invitation is only available between Monday and Thursday commencing 6 October until 27 November, 1980.

£2

Two Pounds

2359

Voucher valid towards one Steak Bar meal only

A 1950's view from Parkhead Road looking towards Bents Road on the horizon. The Wheatsheaf Hotel is on the right. The cottages near to the road have been demolished.

This line of cottages opposite the Wheatsheaf pub were know as Parkhead Cottages. Winifred Wilson (nee Staley) lived in the first one on the left. She remembers taking this photo with her brownie camera shortly before renovation work started. These cottages now house a hairdressers and childrens clothing shop as well as a nursery at the opposite end. Winifred moved only a few hundred yards around the corner onto Parkhead Crescent where she still lives 70 years on.

This photo of the Wheatsheaf Inn and Baines Garage was taken around 1920. The garage was previously a blacksmiths forge but changed to service the age of the automobile. The pub was demolished in 1928. Winifred's brother, Norman Staley, played with his friends on the building site for the new pub that is there today. Norman would tell Winifred stories of large rats to discourage her from playing with him and his friends. Note the two word spelling of 'Wheat Sheaf'.

The track at the side of George Greenfields Post Office
was called Back Lane and went up the hill to Broad
Elms Lane and the fields of Hulley's Farm.
This picture was taken around 1905.

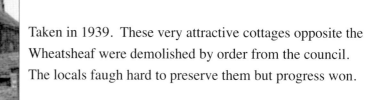

Taken in 1939. These very attractive cottages opposite the
Wheatsheaf were demolished by order from the council.
The locals faugh hard to preserve them but progress won.

14

Parkhead to Silver Hill

10 Alan Ramsey's old house at 331 Ecclesall Road South

11 Holmwood House

12 Ecclesall Manor House

13 Charles Reaney's blacksmiths shop

14 Ecclesall Hall Farm

15 Ecclesall College later Ecclesall Library

Map date 1905

Alan Ramsey built several houses on Ecclesall Road South including the one pictured for himself. Because the land fell away steeply at the back, he was able to build a forty seat cinema beneath the house. He was keen on amateur film making and formed Parkhead Cine Society which was based in the cinema. One of the members, Arthur Humberstone, was a brilliant artist and he helped the society make a feature cartoon film. He went on to work for J.Arthur Rank and later for Walt Disney in Los Angeles.

Arthur Humberstone, seated, at J Arthur Rank Studios.

Aerial View - Ecclesall looking towards Greystones. Hoober Road joins Ecclesall Road, left to right. Holmwood is in foreground. Knowle Lane, Millhouses Lane, Woodholm Road, Silverdale Crescent are in the centre. All Saints' Church can be seen in the distance. c. 1930.

Present day photograph of Ecclesall Manor House. The house has a modern extension and is now offices for several businesses.

Holmwood House was built for wealthy local solicitor Henry Vickers around 1864. He and his wife Sibbilla had two sons and nine daughters. Their eldest son died aged 10, their second son also became a solicitor and lived in the Manor House along the road near Ecclesall Terminus. One of the latest residents to live at Holmwood in 2000 was bass player Rick Savage from local rock band Def Leppard. Holmwood's lengthy drive from Ecclesall Road became Cortworth Road.

The Manor House is set back from the road but

the gate posts leave you in no doubt of its location.

This photo supplied by Gordon Ramsey, shows the blacksmiths shop and Ecclesall Road as a mere track on the right. It was built for the Mottram's, a local family from Hill Top, now known as Bents Green. It was built on waste land at the corner of Millhouses Lane and Ecclesall Road South. c. 1900.

Top of Millhouses Lane as it looks now. Trees are hiding Montgomery Court.

The last blacksmith to work from the site was Charles Reaney. The building was demolished and in 1914. Walter Ramsey bought the land and built a family home.

19

Walter Ramsay with his family and servants at the front of his newly built Montgomery House at Ecclesall Terminus, on the site of Charles Reaney's Blacksmith shop. He sold the house which then became a children's nursery. In 1977 it was demolished and in its place a block of flats was built, which is there today (Montgomery Court).

The builders have stopped to pose for the camera, while the house was under construction in 1914.

There's a lovely story about the Christmas when the tramcars, which had only previously travelled to Banner Cross, finally came up to Ecclesall Terminus – hence the name. Walter who enjoyed a drink or two, put a folding card table at the tram stop with two bottles of whisky and a glass, and a note inviting all the tram drivers to have a Christmas drink on him. Unfortunately, the first driver drank half a bottle, collapsed on the floor of his tram and soon there were trams queued up behind him back down to Banner Cross!

1950's Millhouses Lane looking towards Ecclesall Road South, at Ecclesall Tram Terminus.

Ecclesall Hall Farm, believed to have been built on the site of Ecclesall Hall which belonged to the De Ecclesall family. It later became the home of Gervase Strelley, who in the early part of the seventieth century became Lord of the Manor of Ecclesall. It was demolished in 1935 to make way for new housing.

On the junction of Ecclesall Road and Knowle Lane stood Ecclesall College. It closed in 1880 and the new owner Mr. Crossley renamed it The Knowle. Twelve years later it was bought by John Kingford Wilson who named it Kingscote. Sir William Ellis become the next inhabitant in 1907, it was he who named it Weetwood. He then sold it to Sheffield Corporation in 1945 and it was turned into Ecclesall Library.

Opening ceremony of Ecclesall Library in 1945

The Weetwood House - Restaurant and Bar in 1998

Even though most of the local population wanted to retain their library the city council sold it and in 1998 it opened its doors as a bar and restaurant. This was as unsuccessful venture and in the end the building was demolished and swiss like flats were built, along with a new library.

Inside view of the old Ecclesall Library.

Silver Hill to Banner Cross

16 Banner Cross Road

17 Prince of Wales Hotel

18 Church Parade

19 Ecclesall Church

20 Banner Cross Hall

21 Tram coming up Ecclesall Road South

22 Banner Cross Cottages

23 Cedar Farm House

24 Glenalmond Road

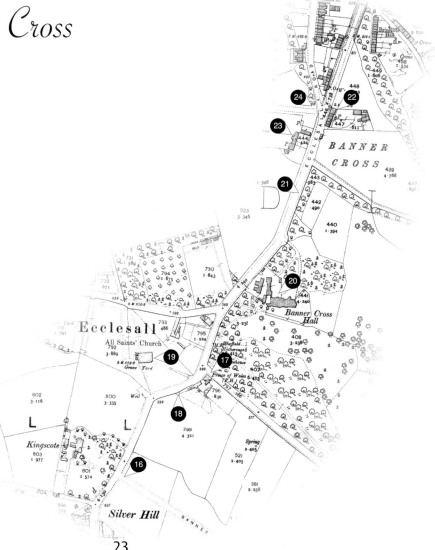

Map date 1905

Walter Ramsay and his family driving up Ecclesall Road South, passing Banner Cross Road.

Tram No. 242 crawling up Silver Hill in the snow with All Saints Church in the background. Surprisingly the snow covered allotments are still there today and not another housing estate built on this lucrative Ecclesall Road site. (Photo taken between 1946-1954)

The Prince of Wales Hotel was built around 1808 reputedly from the stones from the old Ecclesall Chapel. In 1928 it was rebuilt in the mock Tudor style that is present today.

In the 1980s some bright spark renamed it the Woodstock Diner. If that wasn't bad enough it changed its name to the Baltimore Diner then again to the Real Macaw in the 1990s. Finally common sense prevailed and in 1998 it reverted back to its original name.

A late 1980s photo of the Baltimore Diner at No 95, Ecclesall Road South. The junction with Carterknowle Road is on the left.

Church Parade has not changed a lot since this photo from around the mid 1960's. The Chocolate Box and J.W Rose, Bakers are still there today. A film production company had its offices at No.111. The last film to be made just before the outbreak of World War II was called 'Crusaders of Space'. Little did people know that above these shops, futuristic films were being made. Later on, Gordon Ramsey ran his architecture and interior design business from there. He then converted the rooms into a television studio and editing suite in 1979.

The War Memorial in front of Ecclesall Church was erected in remembrance to the people from the parish who lost there lives in both the World Wars. The full list of people can been viewed in the Church. The Prince of Wales public house can be seen in the distance.

Ecclesall Church

In the thirteenth century Ralph de Ecclesall gave his mill on the River Sheaf to the monks of Beauchief Abbey. From the proceeds of the mill the monks were to provide a canon to officiate at daily services in his chapel. These services continued until the Dissolution of the Monasteries in the sixteenth century.

In 1622 the chapel was restored and brought back into use as a chapel of ease to the parish of Sheffield. In the 1780s a new chapel was constructed a short distance away from the old one. This opened on 13 December 1788 and the old chapel was demolished. This building was improved in 1843 and enlarged in 1864. The parish of Sheffield was sub-divided in 1845 and Ecclesall chapel became the mother church of the parish of Ecclesall. A new transept was added in 1907, and the church was reordered in 1964 and 1997.

An artists impression c.1850

Banner Cross Hall dates back to Tudor times. In 1817 the owner General Murray decided to demolish the original hall and build a new one. It was designed by Jeffrey Wyatt a famous architect who worked on Chatsworth House and Windsor Castle.

General Murrey died before its completion and his sister Ann Bagshawe inherited the hall. In the 1930's Charles Boot bought it and is used today as the Henry Boot & Co headquarters.

Early postcard from the 1900s showing a very rural view of Ecclesall Road South looking towards Psalter Lane. A tram stands at Banner Cross Terminus. Cedar Farm can be seen in the distance, on the left.

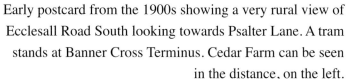

Tram 247 coming up the hill towards Ecclesall Church. Psalter Lane in the distance.

Tram No 290 at Banner Cross Tram Terminus, the start of Ecclesall Road South. The cottages on the right were called Banner Cross Cottages. They numbered 1-11. The end cottage, nearest the camera, is the 'Weigh House', former Toll House. The exact date is unknown but according to records they weren't there in 1795.

Trams, good solid keep left bollards, belisha beacons and mostly pre-war cars characterize this photo of Ecclesall Road, taken on March 21st 1954.

31

Horse Drawn Cart outside Cedar Farm House. The house is still there but the barn joining it was demolished to make way for Banner Cross Methodist Church which is there today. The fields to the left is where Gisbourne Road now cuts across. Taken around 1890.

This popular postcard photo was taken across the road from the opposite photo, except this one is around thirty years older. 1908/9. Psalter Lane in the background.

A happy looking tram driver and conductor at Banner Cross Terminus. Cedar House can just be seen in the background.

c.1910 Glenalmond Road from Ecclesall Road. Banner Cross Methodist Church is on the left. This picture shows very little change over the last 90 years. Every corner did seem to have a confectionery shop on it. This one became a Post Office and is now a travel agency.

1950s Ecclesall Road and Psalter Lane junction from Ecclesall Road South. No 993 was the last building on Ecclesall Road and was the Sheffield Savings Bank.

Banner Cross to Hunters Bar

25 Banner Cross Hotel

26 Where Charles Peace shot and killed Arthur Dyson

27 Greystones Road

28 Ecclesall Road looking towards Greystones Road

29 Carrington Road

30 John Taylor outside No 750

31 Rustlings Road Junction

32 Ecclesall Road looking towards Hunters Bar

33 Toll Gate / Hunters Bar

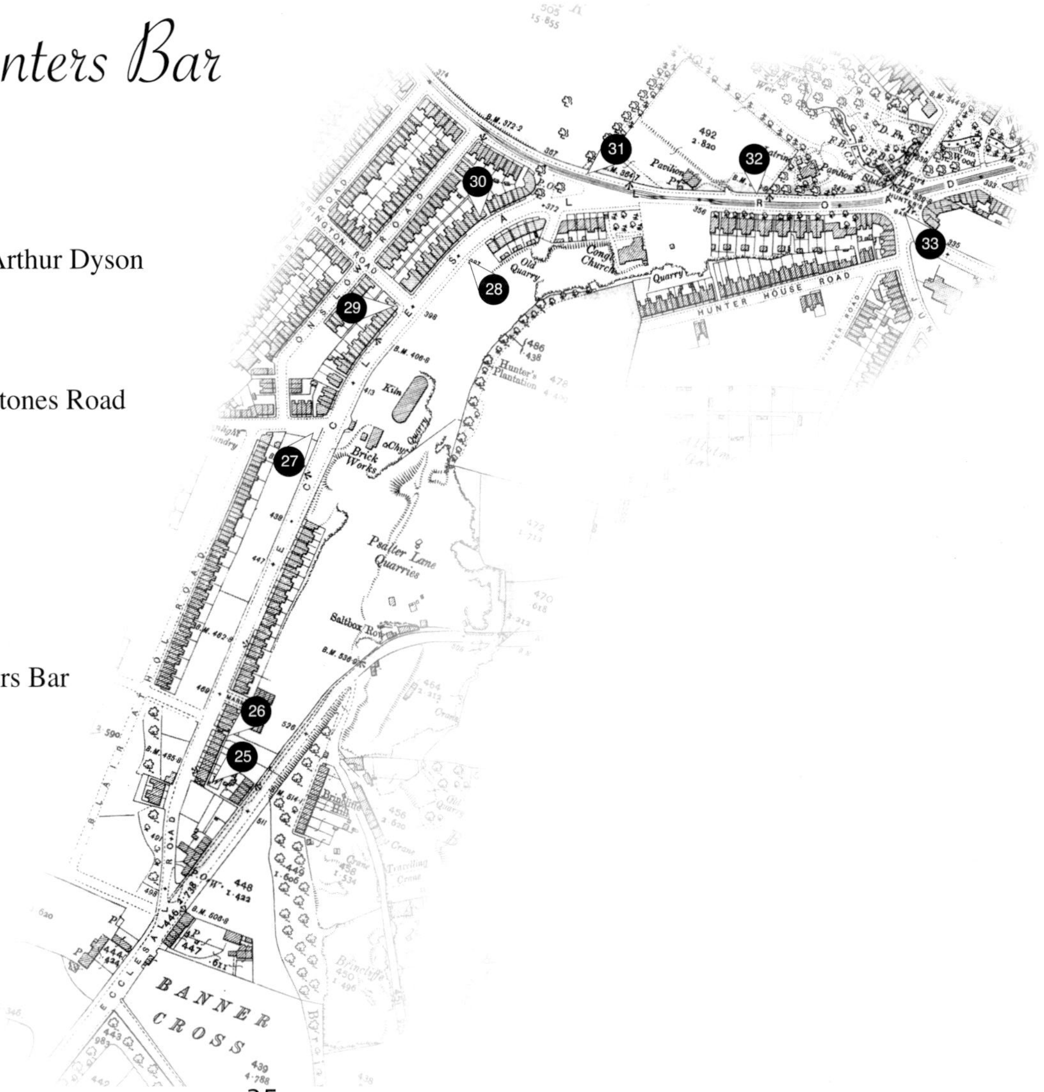

Map date 1905

Walter Ramsay was a big contributor to how Ecclesall Road looks today. He built numerous houses and shops over the years. Walter Ramsay began life mending and selling bicycles and later selling cutlery.

He became a builder by chance, when a customer in his shop said he needed someone to join him in buying a plot of land on which to build houses. Walter put up the money and the houses were built. He decided that this was a much better way to earn a living and from then on he became a builder. He built a row of shops below Hunters Bar and along Sharrowvale Road. The shops at Banner Cross, from 884 Ecclesall Road up to 952, which was a Post Office in the 1930's, now a co-op travel agency. He also built the houses from Dunkeld Road up to Ecclesall Terminus and most of Banner Cross Road.

Beer delivery at the Banner Cross Hotel in 1967. The Landlord / Manager was Alan Coy who later went on to manage The Prince of Wales pub further up Ecclesall Road South. Still serving the best pint of Tetley's in the city, in my humble opinion.

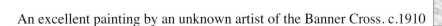

An excellent painting by an unknown artist of the Banner Cross. c.1910

Charles Peace - The Murder of Arthur Dyson at Banner Cross 1876

One evening in October 1878, Charles Peace shot and killed Arthur Dyson at No 951 Ecclesall Road - just below the Banner Cross Hotel.

Peace was born in Angel Court, Nursery Street, Sheffield in 1832. He went to Pitsmoor School and Hebblethwaites in Paradise Square.

Over several years he committed many burglaries and served four terms of imprisonment.

He was involved in a mutiny at Chatham Prison and was deported to a convict settlement in Gibraltar. After his release in 1864 he returned to Sheffield where he set up a picture framing business and later took a shop on West Street.

In 1875 Peace and his wife moved to 40 Victoria Place, Darnall - next door to a Mr & Mrs Arthur Dyson. Peace and Mrs Dyson had an affair. When Arthur Dyson found out he forgave his wife and moved to Banner Cross in the hope of escaping Peace's attentions.

In November 1876, Peace tracked them down and accosted Mrs Dyson in a passage outside there cottage. Her husband came to her aid and Peace shot him. He then fled to London and changed his name to John Ward before setting out on a nationwide life of crime.

He later shot a policeman during a burglary in Manchester and was arrested for attempted murder. His true mame was eventually discovered and he was brought back to Sheffield to stand trail for the murder of Arthur Dyson. He was found guilty and hanged in February 1879.

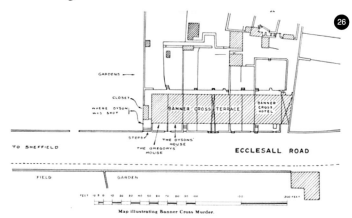

Map illustrating Banner Cross Murder.

c.1920. Looking towards the Brick Works.
No 947 Ecclesall Road on the junction of Marmion
Road can just be seen on the right.
Tram No 301 is in the distance.

c. 1900. Greystones Road from Ecclesall Road
looking towards Greystones School with
A.E. Belton's Steam Lorry in foreground.

The picture house was built by Henry Boot and Sons - a local builder. Mr Rodgers was the owner and his daughter Ethel played the piano to accompany the silent films. The Picture palace closed on Saturday, 17th August 1968. The last film shows were 'A challenge for Robin Hood' and 'Ringo and His Golden Pistol'. This photograph is from the 1980's. The original cinema was then a Bingo Hall and the downstairs ballroom was Napoleon's Casino. The Casino was destroyed by fire in 1982 and the building was later demolished.

Greystones Picture House

Greystones Road, 1895-1915, looking towards Ecclesall Road. Ecclesall Brick Works can be seen in the distance.
Blair Athol Road is on the right.

No's 828 - 782, Ecclesall Road at junction with Greystones Road. No 828, Ecclesall Road, on the corner with Greystones Road was owned by William Hy. Marks, a confectioner.

This pre 1904 picture of Ecclesall Road shows the unmade road and no buildings on the left.

c. 1910 Carrington Road, Greystones looking towards Ecclesall Road. Note the cobble - stoned road. The people in the foreground are very aware of the photographer.

This photo was taken around the mid 30's and is of Roger Taylor's great grandfather John Taylor outside his confectionary shop.

He was born in 1867 and worked at Joseph Rodgers & Sons, cutlers.

He bought the shop for his retirement. I believe, on occasions, he played the organ at St Augustine's church on Brocco Bank.

The number 750 is just discernable above the shop door.

This photo is hanging on the wall of the Porter Brook Public House. It was taken around 1900 and shows a horse and cart heading to Banner Cross. The junction to Carrington Road can just be seen on the left.

44

Ecclesall Road approaching Rustlings Road during the morning rush hour. (1950's) Somewhat different from the twenty-first century bus lanes.

Rustlings Road junction with Ecclesall Road around 1920. Note the horse and cart and the tramcar. Motor cars were very few and far between even in this affluent area of the city. The pedestrians look very well turned out.

The Lord Mayor of London's official visit in 1933.

The procession of carriages are travelling up Ecclesall Road towards Banner Cross and on to the opening of High Storrs School. Their arrival was delayed because the horses found Ringinglow Road too steep and had to go up Bents Road instead.

1920's Ecclesall Road looking towards Hunter's Bar, Endcliffe Park on left.

There are many photo's of Hunter Bar Toll House but this one does capture the character of the period. It was built in 1811 charging a toll to use the easier route to Derbyshire. There are a couple of versions as to who the last payer of this tolls was. One version says it was Reuben Thompson's horse bus which passed through the toll bar, turned around and came back through just after midnight on the 31st October 1884 becoming the first person through the toll free of charge. Other accounts say it was Mr William H Haigh, a cab proprietor who was first. Both accounts say there was a huge cheer from the gathered crowd and shortly afterwards they took off the gates and threw them over the wall into a field, or was it into the dam to the right!

Reuben Thompson's Ecclesall Road horse bus at Hunter's Bar, 1898.

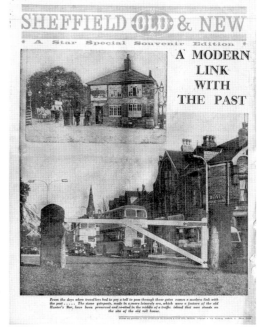

A Star special edition newspaper, dated Saturday June 24th 1961.
Its showing Hunters Bar in the past and what was then the present.

The large house in the background is Hunter House Farm, which became part of The Hunter House Hotel and now is a Buddhist Meditation Centre.

Photograph c.1915. The old Hunters Bar Toll Gate Posts can be seen on the right at the entrance to Endcliffe Park. The posts now stand in the middle of the roundabout that is there today.

1930's Hunters Bar. For a long period there was nothing in the middle of the junction of Ecclesall Road, Junction Road and Brocco Bank. The horse trough in the centre of the road is said to have been put there by the Wilson family from the nearby snuff mill, perhaps in memory of Henry Wilson. To the right you can see one of the famous Sheffield police boxes introduced by Chief Constable Percy Sillitoe in 1928.

Hunters Bar to Collegiate Crescent

34 Woofindin Almshouses

35 Boots Chemist, corner od Neill Road

36 Ecclesall Road at junction with Hickmott Road

37 Wadbrough Road

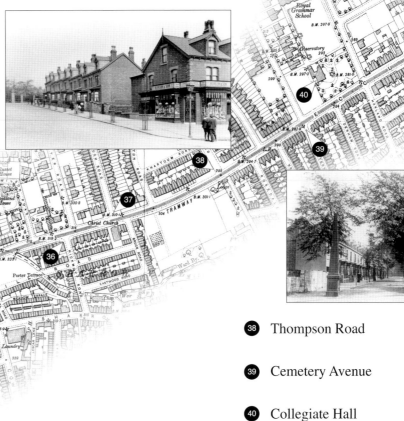

38 Thompson Road

39 Cemetery Avenue

40 Collegiate Hall

Map date 1905

Woofindin Almshouses were built in 1898-99, paid for by a bequest from George Woofindin, a cutlery manufacturer, who also paid for the Woofindin Convalescent Home near Whiteley Woods. There are 18 red brick cottages in a crescent which were used as homes for poor persons of both sexes, 60 years old or upwards. Its a very pleasant setting with the River Porter running through the grounds.

Present day and 1950's Boots Chemists, No 649, Ecclesall Road, at junction of Neill Road. Good to see somethings never change!

c. 1910 Hunter's Bar premises include No 651 G & J.W. Lister, Butchers. No 653, Frederick Loukes, Stationer. No 655, Arthur Blake, Boot Dealer. No 657, Harold H. Greenfield, Chemist. According to the sign on the roof this row of shops was named Endcliffe Market.

Tommy Ward's shop just down from Hunters Bar had an exciting shop window display. If you liked coal that is! It showed the different types available to order. The main three were, coal for cooking stoves, household fires and hot water boilers. I thought coal was coal!

A few people enjoying a drink on a nice sunny day outside Gallery 3, which was on the right hand side near where the Spar shop is today. c. 1978

Hickmott Road c.1900
Nos 541-503, Ecclesall Road at junction
with Hickmott Road, including yet
another confectionery shop,
Mrs Ellen Hadfield at number 541.

Taken from Ecclesall Road
looking up Wadbrough Road.
c.1915. The wall to the
Botanical Gardens can be
seen in the distance.

Photo and the combined advert for the row of shops in the South Sheffield Guardian in April 1984.

Long standing shop owner Don Alexander and his wife outside his shop in 1984. The shop, now run by Paul Iseard, still sells Sheffield made items but is now called 'The Famous Sheffield Shop'. Paul got a petition together and successfully stopped the proposed plan for a McDonalds restaurant in Berkeley Precinct in 2002.

c. 1900 Thompson Road from Ecclesall Road. Entrance to the Botanical Gardens is in the background. No 418 Ecclesall Road is Burgon & Son, Grocers. Note the newly planted trees. Sheffield was noted then for its tree planting - as it still is today - giving us our 'green' city.

c. 1978 Berkeley Precinct before Tesco's expansion and world domination!

Note the left corner of Cemetery Avenue and Ecclesall Road which has yet to be developed. This photo is believed to date around 1903. The two obelisks marked the entrance to the gatehouse of Sheffield General Cemetery.

Ecclesall Road looking towards the city centre. The two obelisks are visible on the right as are the newly built shops and houses. Notice the elaborate posts for the overhead tram wires. The first electric tram route in Sheffield ran from Nether Edge to Tinsley in 1899 - replacing the horse trams. The Ecclesall road route followed soon after.

Collegiate Hall in the early 1900s. Built as part of Collegiate School which was founded in 1836. It later merged with the Royal Grammar School in 1884. It was used during the first World War as a hospital for wounded soldiers. It later became a Teacher Training College and finally merged with Sheffield Hallam University. How modern the architecture of the building still looks - a century later. The junction of Broomgrove Road is hidden by a 'Short Tram' heading up Ecclesall Road.

World War I, bus carrying Belgian causalities entering Collegiate Crescent then a gated road.

COLLEGIATE HALL SHEFFIELD.

Collegiate Crescent to the City Centre

(46) Sheaf Brewery

(41) Collegiate Crescent

(47) The Star Picture House

(42) 259 Ecclesall Road 'Plantation House'

(43) Pomona Hotel

(44) Houses opposite Summerfield Street

(45) Corner of Summerfield Street

(48) The New Inn at the junction of Hanover Street.

(49) At the junction of Moore Street and Hanover Street

(50) Bottom of Ecclesall Road

(51) Midland Bank at No 3 Ecclesall Road

(52) Junction of Cemetery Road and London Road

Map date 1905

c. 1910. The lodge at the bottom of Collegiate Crescent was a private house for many years. Now it houses a student letting company and a hair salon.

Early 1980's photo of this short parade of shops which only Uncle Sams and Sweeny hair salon remains.

1970's Victoria Wine Bar was at No 295 on the corner of Harland Road.

This was a popular meeting place for young people - very fashionable at the time.

Robert Brady's Gentlemens Finery occupied the old Midland Bank building (pictured on Page 75) for a short time before moving onto Ecclesall Road's Golden Mile. Unfortunately no longer there today, now a bar.

Robert Ingram ran his tea merchants business from 259 Ecclesall Road. His business was successful and in 1937 he demolished the building at 259 and had a new building designed and built in its place, 'Plantation House'. It was the first re-enforced concrete building to be constructed in Sheffield. This building still remains, the upper floors now used as offices and the ground floor as a pub.

Robert Ingram began his business much more modestly however, from the house he lived in at 286 Sharrow Lane (see picture). He sold packets of tea, packed by his daughters, from a tray hung around his neck. He progressed to delivering tea by horse and cart and later by sign-written vans. (see picture) Robert Ingram and his wife Edith moved from Sharrow Lane to live on Abbey Lane, just down from Parkhead, where they lived until their deaths.

1970's photo of the Pomona Hotel which was at No 213, Ecclesall Road.

c.1890 Members of Sharrow Cycling Club in the garden of their headquarters at the old Pomona Hotel. Moustaches were obviously in fashion and note the bike with small inflated wheels.

Houses opposite the junction of Summerfield Street. 1895-1915. Is the policeman posing for the camera?

Tram 178 heading out of town. Summerfield Street on the right, Star Picture House on the left. Circa 1950.

Former S.H.Ward & Co. Ltd., Sheaf Brewery before conversion into flats. Summerfield Street and Cemetery Road junction can be seen in the distance. The General Cemetery C of E Mortuary Chapel visible on the skyline. Early 2000.

S.H. Ward & Co. Ltd. Sheaf Brewery.

Jolly Buffer at No.144 in the late 1980's.

Note the artwork, done in brick work depicting a grinder, strangely not a buffer. The only person to ask about this would be the artist Walter Richie but sadly he died in 1997. Tragically his work was lost when the building was demolished.

The Star Picture House was a very imposing red brick building with a domed and colonnaded tower. It opened for Christmas on the 23rd December 1915. The first film shown was 'Marguerite of Navarre'. To mark the occasion people were admitted free for the first performance. Its first sound film 'Under the Greenwood Tree' was shown exactly fourteen years later on the 23rd December 1929. It closed as a cinema on Wednesday, 17th January 1962. The last films shown were 'Voyage to the Bottom of the Sea' and 'Dossier'. The building reopened as a Star Bingo hall until 1984 and was finally demolished in October 1986. A petrol station now occupies the site.

Demolition of The Star Picture House in 1986.

1960's Ecclesall Road and junction of Hanover Street.
The New Inn was demolished in the mid 1980's.

Devonshire Arms Public House, No 118, Ecclesall Road.
The adjoining buildings have obviously been knocked down.
A conservatory extension to the pub now stands where the upholsterer was.

69

Evening Rush Hour, Ecclesall Road - late 1950's

1960's elevated view of Ecclesall Road at the junction of Hanover Street on the first day of the new one way system. No 97, Earl Grey public house is on the right.

1960's photograph of the evening rush hour near Moore Street. Parked cars are creating single line traffic from the City Centre.

Bottom of Ecclesall Road
c.1905.
Good quality shops are
already becoming
established in this up and
coming area of Sheffield.

The members of the Sheffield & Ecclesall Co-operative Society were paid yearly dividends - called the "Co-op Divi". Each member was given a number - this number was handed in with ever purchase made at the Sheffield and Ecclesall Co-op's throughout the year - mainly on groceries from the many Co-op Branches, but also for bigger purchases such as furniture, clothing and bedding etc from the Co-op on Ecclesall Road. You had to collect your dividend in cash from the top floor of the Ecclesall Road shop. A very useful addition to the house - keeping!

Sheffield & Ecclesall Co-operative (The Arcade) on the left.

c. 1965 photo of Midland Bank at No 3 Ecclesall Road. Cemetery Road is on the left. Sheffield & Ecclesall Co-op, The Arcade in the background. The Midland Bank building is the only structure to survive the re-development of the whole area.

This picture really captures what it was like at the bottom of Ecclesall Road around 1905.

This rare photograph shows a busy scene close to the bottom of Ecclesall Road. Note the pointsman's box for the trams, behind the policeman.

Part of the major changes and road works at the bottom of Ecclesall Road with Sheffield & Ecclesall Co-op on the left and St. Mary's Church, Bramall Lane in the background.

c. 1890 Coach and omnibus proprietor William Henry Haigh had his offices at the junction of Ecclesall Road (right) and Cemetery Road (left) - on the site of the later Midland bank. The stabling would be at the back of the building.

A 1960's shot of the roundabout at the junction of Ecclesall Road, The Moor, St. Mary's Gate and London Road.

Other local titles available from Arc Publishing

Sheffield 10
Photographic memories of Broomhill, Crookes and many other suburbs of Sheffield 10. A fascinating look back in time which includes a journey through the Porter Valley.

£8.99

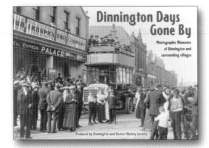

Dinnington Days Gone By
A selection of photographs collected over many years by Dinnington & District History Society. The book shows the growth of Dinnington and the surrounding villages from their early beginnings as farming communities until the latter part of the 1900s.

£8.99

Handsworth in days gone by
by Sandra Gillott
Sandra and the Handsworth Historical Society have put together this fascinating collection of photographs, many from the early 1900's. The local people, transport and buildings are all covered in this new book.

£8.99

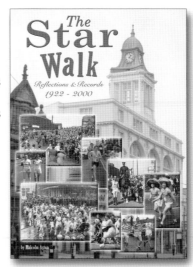

The Star Walk (Reflections & Records 1922 - 2000)
This A4 size book with lots of photos, and information about the famous Star Walk that took place between 1922 and 2000. Many Sheffielders will have fond and nostalgic memories of this great sporting event. Malcolm Ayton author and walker in the races, has combined his recollection of the race with the records of runners over the years to give a fascinating enjoyable book.
£12.99

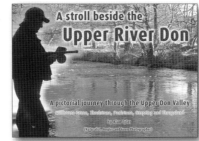

A stroll beside the Upper River Don
A pictorial journey through the Upper River Don from its start at Winscar Reservoir to the village of Thurgoland. The book covers the towns and villages along its path, as well as the beautiful fauna and wildlife.
£8.99

Visit our website: www.sheffieldbooks.co.uk